# BISHOP JOHN

# SEX

# SHOULD WE ◇ CHANGE ◇ THE RULES?

# LET US ARGUE IT OUT

Creation House
Strang Communications Company
600 Rinehart Road
Lake Mary, FL 32746
(407) 333-0600

If the Lord of hosts
had not left us a few survivors,
we would have been like Sodom,
and become like Gomorrah.

Hear the word of the Lord,
you rulers of Sodom!
Listen to the teaching of our God,
you people of Gomorrah!
What to me is the multitude of
your sacrifices? says the Lord....

When you come to appear before me,
who asked this from your hand?
Trample my courts no more;
bringing offerings is futile;
incense is an abomination to me.
New moon and sabbath and
calling of convocation—
I cannot endure solemn
assemblies with iniquity....

Wash yourselves; make yourselves clean;
remove the evil of your doings from before my eyes....

Come now, **let us argue it out,** says the Lord.
though your sins are like scarlet,
they shall be like snow;
though they are red like crimson,
they shall become like wool.
If you are willing and obedient,
you shall eat the good of the land;
but if you refuse and rebel,
you shall be devoured by the sword;
for the mouth of the Lord has spoken.

—*Isaiah 1:9-11,12-13,16,18-20*

# Contents

# Introduction

As the twentieth century comes to a close, the subject of human sexuality in general, and homosexuality in particular, is very much before the Church. Virtually every major denomination in the United States has set up commissions to re-examine questions most people thought had been settled generations ago.

In 1943 popular lay theologian C.S. Lewis thought he was expressing the shared convictions of the great majority of Christians everywhere when he wrote: "There is no getting away from it: the old Christian rule is, 'Either marriage, with complete faithfulness to your partner, or else total abstinence.' "[1]

Lewis quickly added that this was so difficult a standard, and one that was so contrary to our sexual instincts, "that obviously either Christianity is wrong or our sexual instinct, as it now is, has gone wrong. One or the other. Of course, being a Christian, I think it is the instinct which has gone wrong."[2]

Half a century later it seems that many sincere Christians, including many clergy and theologians, have come to the opposite conclusion. They believe that it is not our sexual instincts that have gone wrong, but the Church itself that has been wrong in insisting on such a restrictive understanding of the legitimate expression of sexual intimacy.

Young people mature at an earlier age than they used to. Yet typically—for both financial and social reasons—most put off marriage until a much later date. Under these circumstances, many consider sexual intimacy before marriage to be inevitable.

A divorce rate hovering at nearly 50 percent suggests the probability of multiple sexual relationships before and after marriage itself. Some of these occur during that terrible period of estrangement before the marriage is officially terminated. That used to be condemned as adultery. Today, however, much of the Church, along with society in general, seems to accept it as a legitimate "search for intimacy."

Because of the fragility of contemporary marriages and the devastating consequences of divorce, increasing numbers of Christians are choosing to explore a long-term sexual relationship prior to committing themselves to the "bonds" of matrimony.

For some of our more senior citizens, the tax structures of this country make it extremely disadvantageous to marry, instead of living together as committed but legally single persons.

Far more controversial than any of the questions raised by these societal changes is the debate concerning homosexuality. Until very recently, the Church—and indeed society at large—has regarded homosexual activity as an aberration, a distortion, an illness, a perversion or even an abomination. Today it is widely argued that all such labels and the accompanying attitudes of fear, ignorance and prejudice are the sinful expressions of homophobia.

Growing numbers of people are pressing the argument that no one chooses his or her sexual orientation. Therefore, to deny the legitimacy of sexual relationships to homosexual men and women is said to violate their basic civil rights. For Christians, it is further said to deny them the dignity of their equal standing before God, a denial of the gospel itself.

In the Episcopal Church recent debate has focused on related questions concerning the sexual behavior of those seeking to be ordained. Is it ever appropriate to ordain single persons who are not celibate? If so, under what conditions? For example, if a homosexual man or woman is living in a committed, loving relationship with a same-sex partner, is that essentially different from a heterosexual person living in a committed, loving marriage? If ordination is permissible for the one, why not for the other?

The purpose of this booklet is to address these several, related issues from the perspective of Scripture. I do not speak to the issues on a medical or a scientific basis, although medicine and such sciences as sociology, anthropology and psychology obviously have much to say that will help us understand these complex matters. My purpose is to examine the biblical framework within which insights from the other disciplines can be received, welcomed and evaluated by Christian people who are committed to the authority of God's Word.

I write as a Christian to other Christians and as an Episcopalian to other Episcopalians. My prayer is that God will use this study to help shape and inform the attitudes and decisions of his people as they continue to wrestle with these urgent issues.

# Part One

# Human Sexuality in the Bible

## Jesus and the Authority of the Bible

The question must certainly be asked, where shall we begin such a study? The answer for the Christian is, as always, to begin with Jesus. Jesus himself directed us to do so. "Very truly, I tell you, servants are not greater than their master, nor are messengers greater than the one who sent them" (John 13:16). "Why do you call me 'Lord, Lord,' and do not do what I tell you?" (Luke 6:46).

Jesus' message was as much lived as it was spoken. Clearly it was one of compassion, understanding, forgiveness and reconciliation. He had relatively little to say directly on the subject of human sexuality, and we have no evidence that he ever addressed the subject of homosexuality. However, he did make a number of very pointed comments regarding marriage. In doing so he referred to the purposes of God in creating us male and female in the first place. Against that backdrop, all the questions of sexual behavior must be discussed.

Before turning to these specific comments, however, we must take notice of the still larger frame of reference within which all of Jesus' teaching was couched.

In the Sermon on the Mount especially, and in many other places as well, Jesus made it clear that he presupposed the authority of the Hebrew Scriptures, the books of the

Bible that we call the Old Testament. He considered his own teaching to be an extension and a clarification of the Old Testament, not, as is so often supposed, a radical departure from it. "Do not think that I have to come to abolish the law or the prophets; I have come not to abolish, but to fulfill. For truly I tell you, until heaven and earth pass away, not one letter, not one stroke of a letter, will pass from the law until all is accomplished. Therefore, whoever breaks one of the least of these commandments, and teaches others to do the same, will be called least in the kingdom of heaven; but whoever does them and teaches them will be called great in the kingdom of heaven" (Matt. 5:17-19).

But, it is objected, didn't he then turn right around and set his own teaching in contrast to a whole series of Old Testament precepts? In effect, did Jesus do the very thing he just said he had not come to do? No, even a casual study of the Sermon on the Mount demonstrates that in every instance Jesus sought to clarify the original intention behind a specific Old Testament legal precept. He then set the standard higher than it had been in common Jewish understanding. So Jesus made anger the equivalent of murder, lust the same as adultery, retaliation as bad as aggression and so on.

Jesus did not set aside or lessen the high moral standards of the Old Testament. He endorsed them and made them higher still. Yes, his message was one of forgiveness and reconciliation, thank God, but he never repudiated God's standards as expressed in the Jewish Scriptures. Indeed, in the only recorded instance in which his opinion was asked regarding sexual wrongdoing, his response was, "Neither do I condemn you. Go your way, and from now on do not sin again" (John 8:11).

Further, Jesus promised the disciples that after his ascension he and the Father would jointly send the Holy Spirit to help them recall and understand the things he had already taught them. "The Advocate, the Holy Spirit, whom the Father will send in my name, will teach you everything, and remind you of all that I have said to you" (John 14:26).

Jesus promised that the Holy Spirit would supplement his own teachings with equally authoritative instruction for the church. "I still have many things to say to you, but you cannot bear them now. When the Spirit of truth comes, he will guide you into all the truth; for he will not speak on his own, but will speak whatever he hears, and he will declare to you the things that are to come. He will glorify me, because he will take what is mine and declare it to you" (John 16:12-14).

Clearly the writers of the New Testament understood themselves to be experiencing the fulfillment of this promise as they penned not only the Gospel accounts, but also the Epistles. Repeatedly we read such comments as:

• "Now we have received not the spirit of the world, but the Spirit that is from God, so that we may understand the gifts bestowed on us by God. And we speak of these things in words not taught by human wisdom but taught by the Spirit, interpreting spiritual things to those who are spiritual" (1 Cor. 2:12-13).

• "In former generations this mystery was not made known to humankind, as it has now been revealed to his holy apostles and prophets by the Spirit..." (Eph. 3:5).

• "Now the Spirit expressly says..." (1 Tim. 4:1).

• "And the Spirit is the one that testifies, for the Spirit is the truth" (1 John 5:6).

We begin with Jesus, but almost immediately we discover that we can separate neither his ministry nor his message from the context of the Scriptures as a whole. Jesus endorsed the authority of the Old Testament. He endorsed the New Testament in advance by guaranteeing the Holy Spirit's inspiration to those who were commissioned by God to write it.

This is the reason the Episcopal Church, along with the other churches of the Anglican Communion and virtually all the other branches of Christendom, has always confessed the Holy Scriptures of the Old and New Testaments to be the Word of God. Article XX of the Articles of Religion, written at the time of the Reformation, puts it this way:

> The Church hath power to decree Rites or Ceremonies, and authority in Controversies of Faith: and yet it is not lawful for the Church to ordain any thing that is contrary to God's Word written, neither may it so expound one place of Scripture that it be repugnant to another. Wherefore, although the Church be a witness and a keeper of Holy Writ, yet, as it ought not to decree any thing against the same, so besides the same ought it not to enforce anything to be believed for necessity of Salvation.[3]

Let us, then, examine what both the Scriptures as a whole, and the Lord Jesus in particular, have to say regarding human sexuality.

### Marriage—God's Plan for Sexual Union

**"In the beginning when God created the heavens and the earth...God said, 'Let us make humankind in our image, according to our likeness; and let them have dominion over the fish of the sea, and over the birds of the air, and over the cattle, and over all the wild animals of the earth, and over every creeping thing that creeps upon the earth.'**

**"So God created humankind in his image, in the image of God he created them; male and female he created them" (Gen. 1:1,26,27).**

In this text the intriguing interplay of singular and plural pronouns hints at that great truth that becomes fully evident only in the incarnation of Jesus, namely, that in the singular being of the one and only God there is an interplay of distinct personalities. The one God is somehow more than one. Indeed, as we eventually discover, God is triune. Within the Godhead before the beginning of creation, there was, as St. Augustine put it, an ongoing love relationship: the Father loving the Son, the Son loving the Father, Father and Son loving the Holy Spirit, the Holy Spirit loving the Father and the Son. It may even be said that the creation itself was a kind of overflowing of that love relationship. God created a world and its inhabitants in his image so there would be others with whom he could share his love.

Everything in creation bears some measure of resemblance to God, who created it. "The heavens are telling the glory of God; and the firmament proclaims his handiwork" (Ps. 19:1). But of only one particular creature—"humankind" (*adam* in Hebrew)—does God say, "This is in my own image," that is, "in my likeness." "Humankind" is not "male," but "male and female." Together, in their relationship with each other, male and female reflect something of the nature of God. In the interplay of their maleness and femaleness and in the love for each other which that interplay is designed to express, there is an imaging of the very nature of the triune God.

Note that God gives dominion over the rest of creation equally to male and female. In this initial reference there is no suggestion of superiority/inferiority within the male-female relationship. Rather the relationship is described in terms of mutuality and equality. Shortly, however, through sin this equality becomes horribly marred, but in the very beginning it was clearly there. Neither in the man alone, nor in the woman alone, was the image of God to be seen, but in the two of them together.

**God blessed them, and God said to them, "Be fruitful and multiply..." (Gen. 1:28).**

One of God's express intentions in differentiating maleness and femaleness was that husband and wife might procreate. Just as the love relationship within the Godhead overflowed in the creation of the universe, so in the relationship between male and female the love expressed between them is to overflow in the begetting of children. Their children in turn will be "after *their* likeness." Scripture recognizes, of course, that some people are called to singleness, and that not every married couple will have children. But clearly reproduction was and is a principal factor in human sexuality.

**Then the Lord God said, "It is not good that the man should be alone; I will make him a helper as his partner...."**
**So the Lord God caused a deep sleep to fall upon the man, and he slept; then he took one of his ribs and closed up its place with flesh. And the rib that the Lord God had taken from the man he made into a woman and brought her to the man. The man said,**
**"This at last is bone of my bones and flesh of my flesh; this one shall be called Woman, for out of Man this one was taken" (Gen. 2:18,21-23).**

Sometimes called the second creation story, although scholars debate which is actually older, chapter 2 of Genesis does not merely recapitulate the first account, but rather enlarges upon the relationship between the man and the woman. God initiates the partnership. He fashions the partner. He presents the one partner to the other. Femaleness complements and perfects maleness. Again, as in Genesis 1, there is a full and equal partnership. The term

16

"helper" does not suggest subordination or inferiority in the slightest. Significantly, it is exactly the same term that is used of God himself in such passages as Exodus 18:4; Deuteronomy 33:7,26,29; Psalm 33:20; and so on. If God is our "helper" ("O God, our help in ages past...."), there can hardly be a suggestion of inferiority in calling the woman "a helper as his partner" for the man.

In the man's exclamation that the woman was taken out of himself there is the inescapable implication that they are to be joined together once again—in love, in marriage, in mutuality, in sexual union. "Her bone is my bone, her flesh is my flesh...she is...one with me."

**Therefore a man leaves his father and his mother and clings to his wife, and they become one flesh. And the man and his wife were both naked, and were not ashamed (Gen. 2:24-25).**

The "therefore" in verse 24 makes no sense whatsoever apart from all of the above. Marriage, with its "leaving," "clinging to" and "becoming one flesh," is the logical conclusion to our having been created in the image of God as sexual beings, male and female. In this earliest biblical account, God created human sexuality as a vehicle whereby men and women, created jointly in his image, could experience and express a union called "marriage" in which all of life is shared. Note that this is the account to which Jesus appealed when he addressed these questions. From the perspective of God's intention in creation, marriage is the only context in which sexual union is to be experienced and expressed. Marriage is lifelong, faithful, heterosexual, the commitment of a husband and a wife to each other "in heart, body and mind"[4] that reflects something of the very nature of the triune God himself.

## The Distortion of God's Original Intent

**But the serpent said to the woman, "You will not die, for God knows that when you hear of it your eyes will be opened, and you will be like God, knowing good and evil." So when the woman saw that the tree was good for food, and that it was a delight to the eyes, and that the tree was to be desired to make one wise, she took of its fruit and ate; and she also gave some to her husband, who was with her, and he ate.... Then the Lord God said..."What is this that you have done?" (Gen. 3:1,4-6,13).**

As it always does, temptation began with the challenging of God's Word. How often has the argument been made that if something doesn't harm anyone else it shouldn't be unlawful? The serpent suggested much the same to our first parents. The fruit he urged them to sample, he said, would harm no one. Indeed, it appealed to them on every level of their being: biologically it was "good for food," aesthetically it was "a delight to the eyes," and intellectually it was "desired to make one wise." We can almost hear the couple asking themselves, "How can anything so beautiful be wrong?" The tempter promised that disregarding the explicit commandment of God would entail none of the penalties the Lord had warned them of. No, eating the forbidden fruit, he said, would actually cause them to see themselves in a new way. They would become like God himself. They would know good and evil.

Significantly, God himself acknowledged that the couple had, indeed, come to see themselves in a new way when he asked, "Who told you that you were naked?" God says in effect, "See, they have become like us, knowing good and evil." But the life-and-death issue that frames the whole of the biblical witness, the question that remains before us to this day, is: who was right, the Lord or the tempter? God said, "In the day you eat of it you shall die." The serpent said, "God's a liar; in the day you eat of it you won't die, you'll discover what it really means to live: life lived to the hilt, biologically, aesthetically and intellectually."

Who was right? If we understand "life" to be measured in biological, aesthetic, intellectual terms, the serpent was certainly correct. They ate and they didn't die! Not for years. They had children, grandchildren, great grandchildren....

However, when we begin to understand the way the Scriptures use the terms "life" and "death" we also begin to see the extent of the devastation that ensues from disobedience. Jesus himself said, "And this is eternal life, that they may know you, the only true God, and Jesus Christ whom you have sent" (John 17:3).

Life defined biblically is not primarily biological, intellectual nor aesthetic, although it involves all these dimensions. Life is primarily spiritual: a matter of our relationship with God. Thus, the message of the prophets is not, for the most part: "If you sin, you will die." Instead, one after another the prophets declare, "You are already dead in sins and trespasses, but God will make you live." David prays, "Create in me a clean heart, O God, and put a new and right spirit [or life]—within me" (Ps. 51:10). Isaiah says, "We stumble at noon as in the twilight...as though we were dead" (Is. 59:10). Jesus says to Nicodemus, "You must be born from above" (John 3:7).

The effects of the Fall are pervasive. Not only do they touch every aspect of human life, but in ways we cannot even begin to explore here they also infect and corrupt the whole of creation. (See Rom. 8:18-25.)

One particular consequence of disobedience was the corruption of the relationship between the man and the woman, spoiling the marriage relationship designed by

# SEX: SHOULD WE CHANGE THE RULES?

God.

In the Episcopal Church, the marriage service says, "The union of husband and wife in heart, body, and mind is intended by God for their mutual joy; for the help and comfort given one another in prosperity and adversity; and, when it is God's will, for the procreation of children and their nurture in the knowledge and love of the Lord."[5] All this we have seen in the story of creation. All this was adversely affected in the Fall. In place of mutuality and partnership, male dominance became a reality. We are only now beginning to see what a terrible distortion it is. In place of life-long, faithful union, promiscuity on the one hand and divorce on the other became tragically frequent patterns. Instead of a man leaving his parents and joining himself to *one* wife, the monstrosity of polygamy became commonplace.

The oppression of women by men, even and often especially by their own husbands; the taking of multiple wives, concubines and lovers; the distortion of the sacred mutuality of married sexual intimacy into a male pleasure provided by the subservient female—all this is foreign to God's original creation. All of it is part and parcel of the Fall. Along with all the rest, in place of the male/female relationship that God ordained, "same-sex unions" began to occur.

We must understand the distinctions between sexual activity before and after the Fall, because it is to the pre-Fall order of creation that Jesus appeals in addressing sexual morality. Those who argue that the Bible has sanctioned male dominance and, therefore, cannot be a reliable guide when it speaks to sexual issues seem to have entirely missed this critical point. Yes, it is true, all the way through the Old Testament we have multiple marriages, divorce, concubines and so on, but, in the words of Jesus, "from the beginning it was not so" (Matt. 19:8).

20

Yet, for all of the corruption of God's intention, let us note that even under the Old Covenant adultery, defined as "the taking of another man's wife" (but not "another woman's husband") was strictly forbidden and punishable by death. Even within the framework of distortion, dominance and sexual compromise, there was still the strongest sanction possible against violating at least one aspect of the sanctity of marriage.

It is only within the context of the original mandate of God affirmed and reestablished by the Lord Jesus that we can begin to understand the biblical censure of sexual activity outside of marriage.

## Jesus Raises the Standard

Some Pharisees came to him, and to test him they asked, "Is it lawful for a man to divorce his wife for any cause?" He answered, "Have you not read that the one who made them at the beginning 'made them male and female,' and said, 'For this reason a man shall leave his father and mother and be joined to his wife, and the two shall become one flesh'? So they are no longer two, but one flesh. Therefore what God has joined together, let no one separate." They said to him, "Why then did Moses command us to give a certificate of dismissal and to divorce her?" He said to them, "It was because you were so hardhearted that Moses allowed you to divorce your wives, but from the beginning it was not so. And I say to you, whoever divorces his wife, except for unchastity, and marries another commits adultery."

His disciples said to him, "If such is the case of a man with his wife, it is better not to marry." But he said to them, "Not everyone can accept this teaching, but only those to whom it is given. For there are eunuchs who have been so from birth, and there are eunuchs who

**have been made eunuchs by others, and there are eunuchs who have made themselves eunuchs for the sake of the kingdom of heaven. Let anyone accept this who can" (Matt. 19:3-12).**

The law of Moses, as interpreted by the Pharisees of Jesus' day, allowed a man to divorce his wife for any cause. Note that a wife was not given the same prerogative toward her husband. In disagreeing with such practice, Jesus' appeal was to the original purpose of God in instituting marriage at creation. There *is* provision for divorce, he said, because we live in a fallen world ("because you are so hardhearted"), but the only legitimate grounds for divorce is infidelity. Infidelity breaks the marriage relationship. If it is already broken in fact, it may be terminated legally as well. Jesus does not say that it *must* be terminated; there is still the possibility of repentance, forgiveness and reconciliation.

When his disciples protested that this was an extremely severe standard, Jesus recognized that not everyone could accept this teaching. Even in the new community of the Church there will be those who end their marriages for lesser causes. But to do so is not consonant with God's highest standards. However, he added that those who would live for the sake of the kingdom of God either will live by this standard or they will "make themselves eunuchs"; that is, they will abstain from sexual relations.

These, then, are the only alternatives allowed by the Lord Jesus: faithfulness to one's marriage partner or sexual self-denial.

Following Jesus' own lead and inspired by the Holy Spirit with a further elaboration of this truth, the New Testament writers not only affirmed the Old Testament's narrowly defined proscription of adultery, but they broadened it to include a prohibition of *any* sexual unions outside marriage:

22

• "Shun fornication! Every sin that a person commits is outside the body; but the fornicator sins against the body itself. Or do you not know that your body is a temple of the Holy Spirit within you, which you have from God, and that you are not your own? For you were bought with a price; therefore glorify God in your body" (1 Cor. 6:18-20).

• "Live in love, as Christ loved us and gave himself up for us, a fragrant offering and sacrifice to God. But fornication and impurity of any kind...must not even be mentioned among you.... Be sure of this, that no fornicator or impure person...has any inheritance in the kingdom of Christ and of God" (Eph. 5:2-5).

• "Put to death, therefore, whatever in you is earthly: fornication, impurity, passion, evil desire, and greed (which is idolatry). On account of these the wrath of God is coming on those who are disobedient. These are the ways you also once followed, when you were living that life. But now you must get rid of all such things..." (Col. 3:5-8).

• "Let marriage be held in honor by all, and let the marriage bed be kept undefiled; for God will judge fornicators and adulterers" (Heb. 13:4).

• "Since therefore Christ suffered in the flesh, arm yourselves also with the same intention (for whoever has suffered in the flesh has finished with sin), so as to live for the rest of your earthly life no longer by human desires but by the will of God. You have already spent enough time in doing what the Gentiles like to do, living in licentiousness, passions, drunkenness, revels, carousing, and lawless idolatry..." (1 Pet. 4:1-3).

• "And all who have this hope in him purify themselves, just as he is pure" (1 John 3:3).

It is worth recalling that among the Jews and in the ancient world generally marriages were usually arranged by parents. This is still the case in many parts of the world even today. Sometimes the bride and groom did not see each other until their wedding day. Biblically it simply is not the case—ever—that love, feelings, need, desire, proximity or availability legitimizes sex. Marriage does. Period.

A still more profound reason for protecting the sanctity of sex within marriage is found in Paul's astonishing metaphor in Ephesians.

**Husbands, love your wives, just as Christ loved the church and gave himself up for her.... In the same way, husbands should love their wives as they do their own bodies. He who loves his wife loves himself. For no one ever hates his own body, but he nourishes and tenderly cares for it, just as Christ does for the church, because we are members of his body (Eph. 5:25,28-30).**

Referring as Jesus had to the creation mandate, Paul quotes from Genesis 2, asserting that marriage is a living parable of Christ's love affair, his "marriage," to the Church.

**For this reason a man will leave his father and mother and be joined to his wife, and the two will become one flesh. This is a great mystery, and I am applying it to Christ and the church. Each of you, however, should love his wife as himself, and a wife should respect her husband (Eph. 5:31-33).**

Throughout the Old Testament God presented himself as the husband of Israel. Throughout the New Testament Christ presents himself as the bridegroom who courts and wins his beloved, the Church. He commits himself to her without reservation and he lays down his life for her. As she receives him he "impregnates" her with the Holy Spirit, and he becomes the father of a new creation.

All of this is symbolized in the marriage relationship and

specifically in the physical union of husband and wife (even if they don't realize it; even if they don't have any idea that that's what it means). For Christians—who do know it— taking sexual activity out of the place of sacramental significance that God has given it would be like using the altar and the communion vessels for a drunken orgy.

Playing fast and loose with sexuality, whether in pre-marital relationships, extra-marital adulteries or homosexual liaisons, despises the honor with which God himself has invested it and risks our relationship with Christ. St. Paul wrote to the Corinthians that every other sort of sin is outside the body, but sexual sin is against the body itself. He says, "Do you not know that your body is a temple of the Holy Spirit within you, which you have from God, and that you are not your own? For you were bought with a price; therefore glorify God in your body" (1 Cor. 6:19-20).

# Part Two

# Homosexuality: Biblical and Pastoral Issues

## What the Bible Says About Homosexuality

It is frequently noted that there are only seven explicit references to homosexuality in all of Scripture. But this ignores the fact that the whole of Scripture bears witness to the understanding of human sexuality that we have just summarized. Thus all references to sexual temptation, promiscuity, purity, faithfulness, and so on; *all* references to our bodies being the temple of the Holy Spirit (1 Cor. 6:19); *all* exhortations to "present your bodies as a living sacrifice, holy and acceptable to God, which is your spiritual worship" (Rom. 12:1), to die to sin (1 Pet. 2:24, RSV), to "crucify the flesh" (Gal. 5:24), and so on—all such references must be examined and understood within this overarching biblical framework. Within the biblical framework, all such references pertain as much to homosexual as to heterosexual activity.

When Scripture says flee fornication (1 Cor. 6:18, KJV; cf. Matt. 15:19; Mark 7:21; John 8:11; Rev. 17:2,4; 18:3,9; 19:2; 21:8; 22:15) and when it denounces immorality, promiscuity, lasciviousness and the lusts of the flesh, the backdrop is quite simply that *sexual intimacy is legitimate only within the marriage relationship.* If intimacy with a member of the opposite sex is inappropriate outside of marriage, how much more inappropriate is sexual intimacy with a member of the same sex.

Let us look, then, at those seven explicit references to homosexual activity, bearing in mind the larger biblical context in which they occur.

**I**

**For the wrath of God is revealed from heaven against all ungodliness and wickedness of those who by their wickedness suppress the truth. For what can be known about God is plain to them, because God has shown it to them. Ever since the creation of the world his eternal power and divine nature, invisible though they are, have been understood and seen through the things he has made. So they are without excuse; for though they knew God, they did not honor him as God or give thanks to him, but they became futile in their thinking, and their senseless minds were darkened. Claiming to be wise, they became fools; and they exchanged the glory of the immortal God for images resembling a mortal human being or birds or four-footed animals or reptiles.**

**Therefore God gave them up in the lusts of their hearts to impurity, to the degrading of their bodies among themselves, because they exchanged the truth about God for a lie and worshipped and served the creature rather than the Creator, who is blessed forever! Amen (Rom. 1:18-25).**

Whatever the exact historical circumstances of the Fall, St. Paul makes it clear that all humanity has participated in it. He speaks of suppressing (literally: "holding down") the truth and exchanging the truth about God for a lie. He says we have turned from honoring and obeying God to the foolishness of worshipping idols fashioned after creatures. Consequently, God gave them up to *impurity*—to the dis-

28

honoring of their own bodies. Thus, as we have already seen, one of the outworkings of the Fall was that sexual immorality became a part of the human condition. Paul continues:

**For this reason God gave them up to degrading passions. Their women exchanged natural intercourse for unnatural, and in the same way also the men, giving up natural intercourse with women, were consumed with passion for one another. Men committed shameless acts with men and received in their own persons the due penalty for their error (Rom. 1:26-27).**

One of the expressions of our fallenness, but not the only one, is sexual impurity. One of the expressions of sexual impurity, but not the only one, is homosexual activity.

The passage describes what happens when people rebel against God. The operative word is "exchange":

• they exchange the glory of God for idols (v. 23);
• they exchange the truth about God for a lie (v. 25);
• women exchange natural intercourse for unnatural (v. 26);
• men exchange natural intercourse with women for shameless acts with other men (v. 27).

Some have offered an ingenious interpretation for this passage. They would agree that a naturally heterosexual person who exchanged heterosexual relations for homosexual ones would be guilty of the sin of perversion. However, they would also say there is another dimension to be considered: some are naturally homosexual in their orientation in the first place. They sometimes call this "inversion" rather than "perversion."

For them, it is argued, there is no exchanging of relationships with the opposite sex, because they never had them to begin with, and it would be perversion for a naturally homosexual person to exchange relations with members of his or her own sex for relations with members of the opposite sex.

But this argument ignores everything we have established thus far. The norm for what is natural is not what any particular individual feels about his or her sexual orientation, but the way God has ordered creation. If we allow this argument, we must also say that it applies equally well to everything else that Paul catalogs in his unhappy list of consequences of the Fall: evil, covetousness, malice, envy, murder, strife, deceit, craftiness, gossip, slander, hatred for God, insolence, haughtiness, boasting, rebellion, foolishness, faithlessness, heartlessness, ruthlessness, and perhaps most significantly, the applauding of others who do such things. (See Rom. 1:29-32.)

If it can be natural and, therefore, legitimate for someone to be attracted to members of his or her own sex, why cannot it be equally natural and, therefore, equally legitimate, for someone else to feel inclined to murder, slander, rebellion, ruthlessness and so on?

"Natural" in this passage means "according to nature," and that definition is to be found in God's original creation, not in the ways sin has corrupted creation. Our feelings cannot be our guide here, for they have also been corrupted.

## II

**You shall not lie with a male as with a woman; it is an abomination. You shall not have sexual relations with any animal and defile yourself with it, nor shall any woman give herself to an animal to have sexual relations with it: it is perversion (Lev. 18:22-23).**

Most scholars consider that this passage is the clearest biblical statement forbidding homosexual genital activity.

However, some have argued that what is really being proscribed is either a kind of homosexual temple prostitution or the imposition of sex by one man on another, by one woman on another or by a human being on an animal. In other words, homosexual rape is forbidden, as is bestiality, but, it is argued, a loving, consenting homosexual union is not under discussion in this passage.

On the contrary, the words "as with a woman" clearly suggest that what is all right for a man to do with a woman is not all right for him to do with another man. If we read prostitution into the passage we make it say that homosexual prostitution is forbidden, but heterosexual prostitution is permissible. If we read rape into the passage we make it say that homosexual rape is forbidden, but heterosexual rape is not. Of course, Scripture speaks decisively against both prostitution and rape. These verses say that what is permitted between the sexes in marriage is not permitted between members of the same sex.

## III

**If a man lies with a male as with a woman, both of them have committed an abomination; they shall be put to death; their blood is upon them (Lev. 20:13).**

This passage does not merely repeat the prohibition of the previous one. It adds the very sobering consequence of capital punishment for homosexual activity. For that reason some have ridiculed it as an extreme expression of homophobia.

Others discount the passage by claiming that it is rooted in ignorance. This prohibition, they say, is one instance of many trivial things condemned by the unenlightened writers of the Old Testament, such as eating pork, tattoos or the participation of the blind, lame or hunchbacked in liturgical worship.

Let us make some very important distinctions at this point. There are at least four distinct, though sometimes overlapping, kinds of laws in the Old Testament: moral law, ceremonial law, dietary law and agricultural law. The New Testament removes, or at least qualifies, the specifics of the latter three categories. For example, St. Paul and Jesus himself declare that it is permissible to eat pork and other meats previously banned as unclean. A full discussion of the reasons for these differences between the Old and New Covenants is beyond the scope of this booklet. The point we must consider, however, is that the New Testament never abrogates moral laws of the Old Testament.

Further, the Old Testament regarded certain sexual sins as such serious moral infractions as to be punishable by death. For example, all of the capital offenses listed in Leviticus 20 have to do with sex outside marriage, including homosexual activity. The others include adultery, incest and bestiality.

Twentieth-century American society does not punish any of these activities by death, and I am not arguing that it should. However, the leniency of our society does not diminish their seriousness in the sight of God. In fact, the New Testament says that without repentance and amendment of life these activities lead ultimately to the same end: "the wages of sin is death" (Rom. 6:23).

## IV

**The men of the city, the men of Sodom, both young and old, all the people to the last man, surrounded the house; and they called to Lot, "Where are the men who came to you tonight? Bring them out to us, so that we may know them" (Gen. 19:4-5).**

The earliest explicit reference to homosexuality in the Bible occurs in the strange story of the visit of angels to Sodom in the book of Genesis. The angels, literally "messengers from God," appear to be ordinary men who visit the family of Lot, Abraham's nephew. Lot is characterized as a relatively righteous man, living in a wicked city.

When Lot extends lodging to the visitors, the men of the city gather, demanding that the visitors come out so that they might "know" them. There is no question that this verb was a Hebrew euphemism for sexual intimacy. It is the same word used in Genesis 4:1, "Now the man *knew* his wife...."

Lot was so horrified at the demand that he entreated the men of Sodom, "I beg you, my brothers, do not act so wickedly. Look, I have two daughters who have not known a man; let me bring them out to you, and do to them as you please; only do nothing to these men, for they have come under the shelter of my roof" (Gen. 19:7-8). But the men of Sodom would have none of that. They persisted in their demands until the heavenly visitors struck them with blindness. The following day, after Lot and his family escaped, they destroyed the city.

Some have argued that this homosexual incident really wasn't the issue leading to the destruction of Sodom at all. It was, they say, merely incidental to a pattern of sinful self-indulgence that had offended God. They point to Ezekiel 16:49 which says, "This was the guilt of your sister Sodom: she and her daughters had pride, excess of food, and prosperous ease, but did not aid the poor and needy."

Others have maintained that it wasn't homosexuality, but the proposed homosexual gang rape that was the cause of Sodom's downfall. According to this argument, it was for the purpose of humiliating the strangers—to show them who was boss—that the men of Sodom demanded sexual relations with them. Thus, they say the Lord destroyed the city because of the proposed predatory, promiscuous and violent acts of sexuality, not simply because those acts were homosexual.

But all of this overlooks a very important point: God's decision to destroy Sodom and the surrounding cities was made *prior* to the angelic visit. That's what Abraham's great debate with God was about in the preceding chapter. The messengers were sent from God to warn Lot and his family to flee, regardless of the reception the messengers themselves received.

Let us quickly acknowledge that homosexual activity was not the only sin of Sodom. But the book of Jude asserts that whatever else was wrong in that thoroughly wicked city, at the heart of its rebellion was indulgence in sexual immorality and the pursuit of unnatural lust: "Likewise, Sodom and Gomorrah and the surrounding cities, which, in the same manner as they, indulged in sexual immorality and pursued unnatural lust, serve as an example by undergoing a punishment of eternal fire" (v. 7).

## V

**"Bring out the man who came into your house, so that we may have intercourse with him." And the man, the master of the house, went out to them and said to them, "No, my brothers, do not act so wickedly..." (Judg. 19:22-23).**

If there were any doubt as to the meaning of the word "know" in the Genesis 19 passage, this parallel story in the book of Judges answers it decisively. The word is here translated as "to have intercourse with," which, as we have already seen, is the way it was used in Genesis 4 and commonly in the Old Testament. The point is inescapable: where sexual intercourse was legitimate in Genesis 4, because Adam and Eve had been given to each other in marriage, it was an abomination in Genesis 19 and in Judges 19, and an act of wickedness, "a vile thing" (RSV), because there the relationship is not marital but homosexual.

## VI

**Do not be deceived! Fornicators, idolaters, adulterers, male prostitutes, sodomites, thieves, the greedy, drunkards, revilers, robbers—none of these will inherit the kingdom of God. And this is what some of you used to be. But you were washed, you were sanctified, you were justified in the name of the Lord Jesus Christ and in the Spirit of our God (1 Cor. 6:9-11).**

"Male prostitutes" and "sodomites" are speculative translations. The King James Version renders them "effeminate" and "abusers of themselves with mankind." The Revised Standard Version lumps the two categories together as "sexual perverts." The original Greek may have had homosexual prostitution in mind, that is, sexual activity for payment. However, the words do not necessarily carry that connotation. *Malakoi* means "the soft one" and refers to a male who plays the female role in a same-sex relationship, whether for payment or not. *Arsenokoitai* is "one who lies with a male." It refers to a male who plays the male role in a same-sex relationship, whether he pays for it or not. That these sexual activities are put alongside fornication and adultery indicates that the issue is not one of payment, but rather that all these activities are taking place outside marriage.

Let us also note that it is not only sexual sins which are condemned here. They are listed along with greed, drunkenness, reviling and robbery. The good news comes in the next sentence: "And this is what some of you used to be."

Evidently none of these activities is so binding that they cannot be broken through repentance and the healing power of the Spirit of God.

## VII

**Now we know that the law is good, if one uses it legitimately. This means understanding that the law is laid down not for the innocent but for the lawless and disobedient, for the godless and sinful, for the unholy and profane, for those who kill their father or mother, for murderers, fornicators, sodomites, slave traders, liars, perjurers, and whatever else is contrary to the sound teaching that conforms to the glorious gospel of the blessed God, which he entrusted to me (1 Tim. 1:8-11).**

"Fornicators" is from the Greek *pornoi,* the root word for pornography. The King James Version translates it "whoremongers" and the Revised Standard Version, "immoral persons." "Sodomites" is, once again, *arsenokoitai.*

Some contend that the Bible only proscribes those homosexual activities that are promiscuous, predatory, violent or otherwise perverse. But in the light of the rest of the biblical witness, it becomes untenable to draw these lines. Homosexual prostitution and certainly homosexual rape are both extremely unpleasant expressions of human sexuality. But the larger biblical perspective is that they are but two expressions of homosexual activity, which is itself only one of many forms of sexual impurity that derive from the Fall. And all of them are proscribed by the consistent teaching of Scripture as illegitimate, unnatural corruptions of the creation order of God.

Let us be very clear that what this Scripture addresses is homosexual *activity.* The Bible implies neither criticism nor condemnation of those individuals who have what today is termed a "homosexual orientation," that is, those whose sexual temptations are toward those of the same sex. What the Scriptures address and condemn are lust (homosexual or heterosexual) and homosexual activity, not homosexual temptations.

The question of how, or why, certain people develop an orientation of sexual attraction to members of their own sex is a matter of intense debate among psychologists, medical doctors and behavioral scientists. It will undoubtedly be a considerable time before there is anything approaching a consensus on the subject.

However, it must be said that even if scientific evidence were to conclusively demonstrate that homosexuality is genetically determined, it would not force us to conclude that the condition is therefore "natural" and God-given. Nor would such evidence lead to the conclusion that the expression of homosexuality was morally acceptable. The results of the Fall affect the biological order as much as any other part of the created order. Such a supposed in-born homosexual orientation would not require us to conclude that it is God's gift and his will any more than physical birth defects require us logically to conclude that such handicaps are God's gift and his perfect will for human beings with those conditions.

Scripture may not directly address the orientation of sexual temptation apart from actual homosexual activity. But it calls the person who has that orientation to the difficult path of self-denial, just as it does the unmarried heterosexual.

Indeed, as we have seen, Jesus holds up celibacy as an entirely honorable state, saying there are those who have chosen it "for the sake of the kingdom of heaven" (Matt. 19:12).

## Standards of Sexual Conduct for Christian Leaders

Within the Episcopal Church and many others, recent debate regarding human sexuality has focused on the related question of the qualifications for the ordained ministry.

There are four principal passages in the New Testament that discuss the qualifications for Christian leadership, which obviously speaks to a wider ministry than only that of the ordained but certainly includes it. They are Acts 6:1-8; 1 Timothy 3:1-3; Titus 1:5-11; and 1 Peter 5:1-4.

Each text mentions the requirement of a good reputation. In both 1 Timothy and Titus self-control and self-discipline are listed as prerequisites for leadership. Both passages make it clear that a person's home life and sexual conduct are part of what goes into the matter of having a good reputation. Peter requires that an "elder" (shepherd, pastor) must be an "example to the flock" (1 Pet. 5:3). Both 1 Timothy and Titus insist that if the leader marries he (or she) shall do so only once, appealing to God's original intention in creation regarding the marriage relationship (1 Tim. 3:12; Tit. 1:6).

Thus, it is clear that what God expects of all Christians, he particularly expects of those who accept the calling of Christian leadership. God does not have a double standard, but he expects that the one standard will be lived out as fully as is possible by those who are ordained within his church.

As we have seen, Scripture casts no negative judgment on a person whose sexual temptations are oriented in a homosexual direction but who guards his mind from lust and who chooses a life of celibacy. Indeed, Jesus receives and loves such a person, and there is no reason to deny priestly ordination to that person. The biblical issue is not temptation or even orientation. It is self-control both in the mind and in the body. In light of all the passages we have examined, the conclusion is inescapable that it is not appropriate for the Church to ordain anyone engaging in sexual relationships outside the covenant of marriage.

### The Pastoral Task Before the Church

We have summarized briefly, but completely, the biblical basis for the traditional Christian understanding of human sexuality. God's highest and best for his people in the realm of sexuality has always been: *either complete sexual faithfulness within the marriage of one man to one woman, or abstinence from sexual activity.*

A generation ago this would not have needed to be said. Nearly everyone knew these things, and the vast majority of people in America, whether Christians or not, at least paid lip service to them. How society has changed since then!

In 1948, Alfred Kinsey published the first volume of his *Report on Human Sexual Behavior,* and we are still experiencing its massive repercussions. In the early 1960s, Hugh Hefner began cranking out his "Playboy Philosophy," and he once commented: "Here [in the Kinsey report] was indisputable scientific evidence that our entire society was living a lie."

Prior to Kinsey most people claimed to believe in the biblical rule against sex outside marriage. But now there was statistical evidence that what people *said* about sex and what they *did* were two entirely different matters.

In spite of the fact that society resoundingly condemned sex apart from marriage, 85 percent of the men surveyed admitted to having pre-marital sexual experiences and fully 50 percent of them admitted to extra-marital affairs. The statistics on women, published five years later, were not as high, but perhaps were even more shocking. While it might have been all right for young men to sow their wild oats, it was unacceptable for young women to do likewise. "Good girls don't," it was said, but Kinsey demonstrated that good girls did, nearly as often as their male counterparts.

Ironically, contemporary scholars have repudiated many of Kinsey's findings. They say his conclusions were distorted because a preponderant number of the people he studied were sexual deviants. Some say, for example, that Kinsey's estimate that 10 percent of the population are homosexual was exaggerated and that the number is actually closer to 3 percent. However, the Kinsey report worked like a self-fulfilling prophecy, generating an age of sexual license. The damage is done, and some of Kinsey's observations, however untrue at the time, are now being realized.

The traditional arguments against sex before or outside marriage were three: unwanted pregnancy, disease and social stigma. As some wag once put it: "conception, infection, detection."

The modern myth is that we have eliminated these problems. No need to fear unwanted pregnancy. We have the pill, and failing that we have abortion. No need to fear venereal disease. Penicillin and other wonder drugs have finally brought that under control. No need to be concerned about the social stigma. There simply isn't one anymore.

All three statements are lies, of course. We may have the ability to prevent unwanted pregnancies, but we certainly are not doing so. In spite of numerous forms of birth control and more than a million and a half abortions per year, in many of our major cities there are more children born to unmarried teenage girls than there are to older married women. In spite of penicillin and other wonder drugs, venereal disease is at an all-time high. On top of that we now have the AIDS epidemic, a disease without a cure. In spite of widespread acceptance of sex outside marriage, there are still families, communities and churches that find it scandalous.

40

Nevertheless, the myth persists. The argument following from it asserts that, since we have eliminated the three great problems associated with sex outside marriage, the ethic that was based on the fear of these problems is also eliminated.

Premarital intercourse, far from being condemned, is being recommended by authorities as renowned as Dr. Albert Ellis and even by some theologians and clergy. After all, it is asked, how do you know you really love somebody until you have slept together? Some marriage counselors, both inside and outside the Church, actually recommend adultery. Usually they don't call it that. "Open marriage," "sex therapy" or "a little harmless diversion that will help you get in touch with your real feelings" are some of the stock phrases.

Paul Goodman, the brilliant author of *Growing Up Absurd,* sums up the growing no-holds-barred consensus: "In sex, anything you get pleasure from is good, and that's all there is to it."

Over against that mentality is it any wonder that we are witnessing the phenomenon of a "gay rights movement"? If people have little or no choice in their sexual orientation, it is argued, how can anyone deny to homosexual men and women the right to express their sexual desires and needs just as everyone else seems to be doing?

The pastoral task is formidable, indeed. If the church of Jesus Christ is to be true to its Lord, true to its Scriptures and true to its own heritage, there must be a wholesale recapturing of a perspective that has been almost entirely lost in the past half-century. God gave sexuality to human beings not merely as a vehicle for expressing their biological and emotional needs. He created sexuality as a means of expressing within the marriage commitment the union that is possible when a man and a woman pledge themselves to each other "...for better or for worse, for richer or for poorer, in sickness and in health, to love and to cherish, until we are parted by death."[6]

Adhering to this standard is not a matter of condemning those who are not living by it. It is a matter of declaring with love, understanding and sensitivity that God's highest and best in the area of human sexuality is faithfulness within marriage, one man and one woman, and abstinence outside of it.

None of us is perfect, and few if any have an unblemished record in matters sexual. As we come to understand the high calling of God to present our very bodies as living sacrifices (Rom. 12:1), there will be a need for repentance, confession of past failure, the mending of patterns of behavior contrary to God's will, and the loving, caring support of the Christian community.

Homosexual persons who want to conform their lives to the Christian sexual ethic need more than right teaching. Knowing biblical truth is the first step, but knowledge alone is not enough to set anyone free. People in the throes of sexual immorality require much more help. Jesus himself brings freedom and healing to homosexuals, but his grace is mediated through compassionate ministry, teaching, professional counseling, prayer for healing, the sacraments and so on. The homosexual's healing process is not easy. It takes time and patience and the care of many brothers and sisters. A growing number of ministries in the Church are offering hope to homosexuals through programs that provide such care. *Exodus International* (P.O. Box 2121, San Rafael, CA 94912; telephone 415-454-1017) is an umbrella organization for such ministries. In the Episcopal Church *Regeneration* (P.O. Box 9830, Baltimore, MD 21284-9830; telephone 301-661-0284) is a particularly effective ministry.

The origins of homosexual orientation are complex and still under intense debate. Lifelong celibacy is an arduous

_Homosexuality: Biblical and Pastoral Issues_

calling to self-denial, and the admonition to appropriate God's power and grace to change one's sexual orientation is certainly a challenge of faith. Homosexuals often find it hard not to resent such a demand being made of them by heterosexuals who are at least potentially free to express and enjoy their sexuality within the marriage relationship. Discussion of all these matters needs to take place within a context of mutual respect, mutual repentance and the sharing of burdens—in short, within the Christian community as it is called to function by its Lord. Heterosexual persons must not speak to or about homosexuals from a position of self-righteousness or superiority. But for the grace of God in Christ, none of us can stand.

If we are to take seriously the call of God, we must welcome and affirm "all sorts and conditions of men and women." Ours is not a gospel of condemnation, but of new life and forgiveness. Those who are trying with the help of God to live a life that is pleasing to him, no matter how seriously they have failed in the past, must have the whole-hearted encouragement of the Christian community. The adulterer who has given up adultery, the promiscuous person who has turned from promiscuity and the homosexual person who has turned from homosexuality and chosen celibacy—all of these need the understanding, love, prayer and support of the Christian Church, as together we strive to become all that the Lord Jesus desires us to be.

43

# Notes

1. C.S. Lewis, *Mere Christianity* (New York: The Macmillan Company, 1952), p. 81.

2. Lewis, p. 81.

3. *The Book of Common Prayer* (BCP), p. 871.

4. BCP, p. 423.

5. BCP, p. 423.

6. BCP, p. 427.

"Bishop Howe wants the Church to argue out its present dispute over sexual ethics. He presents the full range of biblical texts that must be taken into account if that argument is to be formed by the witness of Holy Scripture. Bishop Howe's account of this witness is clear and provocative. His work will provide congregations an important resource for the argument that indeed ought to take place."

—Philip Turner
Professor of Christian Ethics
General Theological Seminary
New York, NY

"The strength of Bishop Howe's study is its Christ-centeredness. He can interpret particular passages in the light of the whole Bible's compassionate, positive and consistent teaching on God's intentions for human sexuality."

—David A. Scott, Ph.D.
Professor of Ethics
Virginia Theological Seminary
Alexandria, VA

"Finally! A sane biblical approach to the matter of human sexuality. I recommend that this booklet be placed in the hands of each Episcopalian—especially the young."

—Rev. Charles M. Irish
National Coordinator for
Episcopal Renewal Ministries
Denver, CO

"An excellent primer addressing the biblical view of sexuality. *Sex: Should We Change the Rules?* is a welcome addition to the Church's discussion of these issues. I found the beginning strong and extremely balanced and the creation and fall framework very helpful. The outline and explanation of individual biblical passages is particularly useful for clergy and lay alike."

—Rev. Mary Hays
Assistant Professor of Pastoral Theology
Trinity Episcopal School for Ministry
Ambridge, PA

"A thorough and sound biblical discussion of the sexuality issue along with sane, common sense conclusions."

—John Guest
Missionary Evangelist
St. Stephen's Church
Sewickley, PA